WEST END FINAL

HUGO WILLIAMS

West End Final

faber and faber

First published in 2009
by Faber and Faber Ltd
Bloomsbury House
74–77 Great Russell Street
London WC1B 3DA

Typeset by Faber and Faber Ltd
Printed in England by T. J. International Ltd, Padstow, Cornwall

ACKNOWLEDGEMENTS

Some of these poems appeared in *City Lighthouse, Independent, Guardian,
London Magazine, London Review of Books, Observer, Pen Pusher, Poetry
Review, Rising* and the *Times Literary Supplement*. 'Reckless Records' was
commissioned by the *Guardian* and printed as 'In Honour of The Voice
(Frank Sinatra, 1915–98)'. 'Slapstick (Joseph Grimaldi, 1781–1837)' was
commissioned by the Salisbury Festival. 'A Suitable Cane' is part of a longer
poem commissioned by Arts Council England to mark the bicentenary of the
Abolition of the Slave Trade. I would like to thank Neil Rennie, Colin Falck
and Michael Hofmann for their help and support.

A CIP record for this book
is available from the British Library

ISBN 978–0–571–24593–2

Contents

Peach

What were we thinking about
when we climbed up into the fork
of the lookout tree
and kicked the ladder away?

It was almost impossible to get down.
That was the whole point.
We wanted to eat a peach somewhere interesting.
We wanted to dribble peach juice on the world.

A Gap in the Hedge

We go back a long way, you and I,
through a gap in the hedge, across a field,
through a gate we forgot to close,
to a farm museum, where we took off our shoes
and put on protective clothing
to enter the grain silo. A storm of grass filings
broke over our heads. We tumbled around
inside a giant vacuum cleaner,
until we were spat out, blinking in sunlight
to face our accusers. A valuable herd of cattle
had escaped into a neighbouring field,
where they gorged on poisonous berries.

Leaving London

On my way to the ends of the earth
I saw myself going past
in the opposite direction,
heading back into town
through burning stubble fields.
Instead of entering the long tunnel,
I was pole-vaulting valleys,
wire-walking powerlines
over reservoirs, dawdling for seconds
in deserted allotments.

Suburban stations waved me through
with a rush of time in the face.
People and places I remembered
were lit up like tableaux
beside the track.
Flagship office blocks with logos
lurched silently towards me,
then staggered off into the blue.
Buses reappeared with the names
of familiar destinations.

I was hurtling backwards
in a machine of my own making,
feet braced against the seat opposite
as I re-entered the blurred city.
Now here was the OXO Tower
standing out against the night,
streets of shops disappearing under bridges,
a half-curtained window,
lit by a single naked bulb,
almost within reach of my hand.

Heavy Father

When he jumped down from the train
as con-man Tony Gracey
in Michael Balcon's *Rome Express*
I reached out a hand to steady myself.
I was old enough to be his father.

He lights a delinquent cigarette
in the shade of his fedora
and glances up and down the platform,
smudges of mascara visible
under each narrowed eye.

In *One of Our Aircraft is Missing*
he is actor Frank Shelley,
wireless operator on B for Bertie,
disguised as a Dutchwoman.
He raises one eyebrow in the mirror,

or stands looking out of the window
as Sir Robert Chilton in *An Ideal Husband*,
twisting his signet ring round
with circular reasoning,
all other action having cancelled itself out.

How to play anything
from dainty blackmailer to ruined politician
without his assumed character
affecting his performance in any way
was a trick he passed down to me.

How he achieved the transformation
from juvenile lead to Heavy Father
without the use of wigs and make-up
is the great mystery
that is currently being revealed to me.

Elsie Byers

The little pop-eyed goddess
with fists clenched against the sky
he named after Elsie Byers, his American agent,
and placed on his desk
'where I can keep an eye on her'.

His fortunes took a turn for the worse
and we had to move house, but before we left
we buried Elsie under a tree in the garden
to stop her following us.
All would have been well

if I hadn't gone back to the house
to see how Elsie was getting on
in her confinement. There she was,
still buried under her tree,
her mouth stuffed with earth and leaf mould.

One of her eyes was missing.
One of her arms hung loose.
What possessed me to take her home with me?
As I hold Elsie in my hand, I shiver slightly
at the undiminished fury of her scream.

West End Twilight

Hugo Williams sits looking somewhat
cowed and apprehensive in the tea rooms
of the Waldorf Hotel. His appearance, dark,
formal suit and tie, silk handkerchief
arranged for show in his breast pocket,
makes him look old-fashioned actorish.
It is almost as if he were costumed
for a funeral service, and in a sense he is.

Old theatrical aficionados of English
drawing-room comedy and older followers
of old movies where pukka chaps had stiff
upper lips and stiff moustaches, the whole
upper-class apparatus from top hats
to gardenias in the buttonhole, will remember
his father, the actor and playwright
Hugh Williams, whom he writes about so affectingly.

The actor first flared in Hollywood in the 30s,
disappeared into the Army for the duration
of the war, then re-emerged suave and grey
as actor-author, presiding over the drinks tray
in a series of debonair light comedies,
which allowed him to play himself
in the world he knew best – a forgotten world,
which has been re-created here by his son.

Ransacking old letters, he has raided the past
to imagine himself into his father's life
and personality. As the lives of father and son
loom clear, perception of the past is altered.
Reflections shimmer back and forth
as we watch Hugo Williams strolling through
the long twilight of upper-middle-class
light comedy, arm in arm with his son.

Germany

In bed with a temperature
and a case of the wheezes,
I heard the insect whine
of Spitfires and Mosquitoes.

That was my father up there,
wielding the big two-handed
Dettol bottle sword
against hordes of invisible germs.

As Good as New

What a relief to see our Beerbohm caricatures
still hanging in the dining room
and the dining table still there
with the extra leaf being used.
The Regency chair I broke has come back
from the repairers as good as new.
The Copenhagen china hasn't been auctioned off
to keep us at school.
Place-mats of London theatres
are laid out ready for the next meal.

Best of all, the Marie Laurencin self-portrait
didn't go down with the rest of the stuff
on its way to Portugal. Its brown smudges of eyes
look out across the fields
as if they were looking into the future.
One of our old musicals is playing
on the broken radiogram –
Wonderful Town or *The Pajama Game*.
I lean on the back of the sofa
and practise the Charleston.

The Mouthful

Flights of steel-tipped arrows
pass across my father's face
as he looks around the table.
His widow's peak is pulled down
like a Norman helmet.
His eyes are shrapnel.
His irises are wearing
little white spectacles of bacon fat
to examine my plate.

He tells me it's rude
to push my food around
and make dams out of mashed potato
when other people are eating.
He has loaded his fork
with a top-heavy parcel
of peas and lamb,
mint sauce and redcurrant jelly
and hoisted it to his lips.

He tips his head to one side,
as if he is listening,
shuts his eyes for a moment
and lets his jaw go slack.
It quivers slightly as it opens
to allow the mouthful to go in.
I clench my fists under the table,
drawing strength from a fly
that is sitting feeding in his parting.

The Reading

If I turn round now
I'll be back at school,
arranging the chairs in the Library
with Briggs and Napier.
Briggs is chair monitor for readings.
He's flicking through a copy of my new book,
An Actor's Life for Me,
and making rude noises.
A display card on the table
shows me holding up
the Queen's Gold Medal for Poetry.

They have taken me down to the gym
and put me inside the horse.
They push it across the splintery floorboards
while I run along inside,
looking out of the hand-holds,
trying to stay upright
as it crashes into a wall.
Photos of me with the Queen
are floating in the bath
when they force my head under
and hold it there.

Ghost Train

We disappeared into tunnels, sucking sweets,
out-staring our tears
in the darkened windows
of third-class carriages.

How long ago and far away we look,
sitting together there without moving
in the dark train
that is travelling beside our own.

Spin the Board

I have disentangled my limbs
from a crowd of small boys
sitting or lying about
on mattresses in the gym

and hurled myself back
into the noise and light
where Ashley or someone
has given the bread-board a spin

and calmly stands there
waiting for it to run down
to its last few resolutions
before calling out my number.

Not for the first time
in this repetitive game
have I gone into a dive
across the floor of the gym,

one arm stretched out
to try and get a fingernail
under the edge of the board
before it rattles to a standstill.

Egg and Spoon Race

Look out! Look out!
Here come the parents,
the mad delivery boys,
holding out to us in spoons
the sum of all they know.

Their eyes pop out of their heads,
they bite their tongues,
in a desperate effort
to place something
infinitely precious in our mouths.

Twins

I looked up from my plate
and saw the ghost
of my father's smile
separating like milk
across the dining table.

I sat there as usual,
a fork in one hand,
a knife in the other,
and neatly, precisely,
divided myself in two.

And God Created Woman

What rotten luck about the play!
But don't worry,
as soon as I got the news
Flower said I could go out with him,
so we changed into his jeans
and practised archery.

Today we have Television.
Next week we have *Scott of the Antarctic*.
You'll really like Flower when you come down,
but if you see him,
don't say anything about the gang,
as we aren't sure about it yet.

I enclose the End of Term Arrangements,
although I realise it's a bit premature.
Only another thirty-two days
and I'll be free to run around
annoying you all again.
Have we got a new house yet?

I don't mind if we haven't,
because I'm dying to be on my own
and watch television.
If there's time in London when we break up
can we go and see Brigitte Bardot
in *And God Created Woman*?

A Suitable Cane

There is a knock on my door
and Church is standing there,
holding up a ten-shilling note.
'Do you know what this is for, H. Williams?'
He wants me to go to Thomas's the hairdresser
to buy a suitable cane with which to be beaten.

At Thomas's I ask to see a selection
and the old gentleman takes down
various items for my approval:
the knobbly 'School' cane,
the curve-handled 'Pop' cane,
the straight but bendy 'House' cane.
I can't make up my mind.

After supper I am called to the Library,
a book-free zone, plastered with nude pin-ups
of French and Italian starlets.
The House Debating Society
is sitting round on sofas,
pretending to read newspapers with holes cut
    in them.

Church conducts the proceedings,
flexing the cane I bought for him earlier.
'You were seen in O'Sullivan's Record Shop
dancing the Charleston.
Perhaps you'd care to demonstrate?'
He puts on 'Good Golly Miss Molly' by Little
    Richard.

'All right, you can stop doing that now.
Put your head under the table.'
He flicks up my tails with his cane,
takes aim with a little tap.
The whirr of air, the sudden punctuation mark.
And then the absorption, the storing away
of anything like tears or cries,
as if for later use.

Slapstick
(Joseph Grimaldi, 1778–1837)

I was no sooner born
than bouncing off the walls
of Sadler's Wells
whirled round the head of my father,
an Italian dentist
turned ballet master,
till one day the chain broke
and Little Joseph Grimaldi
went flying away from his father
into the arms of a spectator.

Grimaldi Senior's low comedy clown,
constantly falling down drunk,
unable to express himself
except in the language
of violence and sex,
was too much, even for his son.
I found I had a flair
for parental caricature,
dressing up and spouting
nonsense at everyone
in cod Italian.
'I am Grim-all-day,'
I told my hangers-on,
'but I make you laugh at night.'
When the old man caught me
making fun of him backstage,
he beat me savagely,
put me in the monkey's cage
and hoisted me into the flies

to cool off – an act of cruelty
which brought on his own
death from apoplexy.

Now it was up to me
to put aside childish bruises
and step into my father's shoes.
I would soon be recognisable
as 'Senior Guzzle',
swigging from a whisky bottle,
swaggering about the stage
gobbling strings of sausages,
trays of jam tarts with lashings
of whipped cream on top,
dishing out slapstick thrashings
to anyone who tried to stop me,
falling down and being arrested.

I would come on as Sir Feeble Sordid
in a post-chaise constructed
from a wood basket
and two cheeses, my coat encrusted
with frills and spots in the manner
of my failed dandy father.
In coal scuttle 'boots'
and candlestick 'spurs'
I drilled officers
of a swell cavalry regiment
with such an air of hauteur
that a note was sent to the Manager
threatening withdrawal of the Royal Warrant.
In a duel 'to the death'

myself and opponent
shot our seconds with blunderbuses
and shook hands over the corpses.

In mid-life, spasms and cramps
crept over my performance.
Every bone in my body had been broken
at least once
in the countless comic kickings
and pratfalls undertaken
in the name of comedy.
'I am Grim-all-day,'
I told my audience,
'so why do you laugh at me?'
Reduced to performing in a chair,
I consulted a doctor,
who took one glance
at my doleful countenance
and referred me elsewhere.
'There is only one thing for you, sir.
You must go and see Grimaldi the Clown.'

My days of laughter long gone,
I lingered for a while
in the inglenook
of my local hostelry,
carried home each night
on the back of the landlord William Cook,
to my lodgings in Southampton Street,
where only my frolicsome
breeding pigeons fluttered a welcome.

No Disrespect

As for your dad, while being terribly impressed by him,
I was also sort of horrified. It sounds stupid,
but he was always so exactly the same every night.

How could he say the same lines the same way
eight times a week for a year and never miss a beat?
After six months, I longed to run on and speak
    Mandarin

to see if he would react any differently.
I suppose I knew he fancied me – a twinkle in the eye –
but it wasn't until we did a TV together a year later

and he offered to drive me up for the recording
and have dinner together (we were staying in the same
    hotel)
and I declined, that I realised he was serious.

His impeccable veneer didn't crack and after a while
we got over the hiccup. But things were never quite
the same between us. No disrespect to Tam,

but he, Kenny More, Richard Todd, Jack Hawkins,
were the 'old school' – totally disciplined of course,
but sometimes at the cost of innovation and spontaneity.

Academic

I think of him smoking rather well
in plays of his own making,
tapping his cigarette on the box
in the manner of his day,
drawing back his lips
as revival withered him.
He could light his own cigarette,
but he needed a man, he said,
to look after his lighter,
and my mother was always there.

Poems to My Mother

You're the top, you're an ocean liner.
You're the top, you're Margaret Vyner.
– COLE PORTER

1 *The Cull*

You sit with your address book
open on your knee,
gently but firmly
crossing out the names
of old friends who have died.
'I wonder what happened
to Kay Morrow?' you ask.
'It doesn't matter,
I never liked her really.'
Your pen hovers briefly
over the head of the bridesmaid
we've heard so much about,
then slices her in two.

You have the look of a job well done
as stragglers are rounded up
for demolition.
'Dear old Denny Moon!
He taught me to ride.
He used to jump out from behind a tree
cracking a banksia whip.
That, or driving an old Lancia
between kerosene tins.'
You shake your head at him.
In spite of all the fun
you smile with quiet satisfaction
as you let him slip away.

2 New South Wales, 1920

A hundred miles ahead of the drought
and behind on the payments
you were on your way
to start a new life in New South Wales
when the car broke down
under a coolabar tree
and your father said it was The End.

He made you get down
and wait in the shade of the tree
while he went and stood on his own.
You thought you had arrived in New South Wales
and could start to explore,
till you looked behind the tree
and saw the bush stretching away.

He brought your luggage over
to where you were sitting
and started sprinkling petrol over the car.
You thought he was cooling it down
and giving it a clean,
before you set out once more
for your new life in New South Wales.

3 Only Child

Your front wheel runs ahead of you
through the yew tree tunnels.
The berries lie in your path,
like days for you to thread.

You jam your brakes
and fly ahead of your plans.
Your elbows are grazed.
Your handlebars are askew.
Someone has to straighten them for you.

4 *Someone's Girlfriend*

I'd met him before, of course, at somewhere like
Government House in Sydney, then again
in a nightclub in Le Touquet, doing my nut
trying to get him to light my cigarette.
I'd heard he was going to be in this
Freddie Lonsdale play on Broadway, *Half a Loaf*,
so I got my agent to fix me an interview
with the director, Gilbert Miller,
who threw me the part of someone's girlfriend.
When your father saw me sitting there
in the dining room of the SS *Washington*,
drinking my glass of milk, he thought he'd just
discovered me. He sent a note to my table
saying 'Champagne better than milk,
why don't you join me?'
                        I remember it was evening
when we arrived in New York harbour.
Guy Middleton and Frank Lawton came down
to meet the boat in their dinner jackets
and took us back to a party. Your father and I
were staying at the Gotham, but it wasn't long
before we moved to the Devil, which was just as well,
I suppose, considering he was still married.

5 *Café de Paris, 1940*

I borrowed this totally embroidered
low-cut figure-hugging dress
for some charity do at the Café de Paris.
I was there to be decorative
and pose with a white pekinese,
while Lucienne Boyer sang 'Parlez-moi d'amour'.
Esmé Harmsworth won the tiara,
or someone gave it to her.

Oh, and I'll tell you who else was there,
Douglas Byng, 'The Cock of the North'.
He came on in this terrible kilt
with his usual monocle and twitch
and sang 'Flora Macdonald'.
Then there were The Yacht Club Boys:
'The huntsman said he'd found the scent.
We wondered what the huntsman meant.'

We all had to go up on stage afterwards
and Tony Kimmins, he was the organiser,
trod on my train, which immediately came off,
revealing the backs of my legs.
I let fly with a stream of invective,
which everyone heard apparently.
Tony always said he hadn't realised I was
Australian until that moment.

6 *A Conjuring Trick*

The undertaker slips me a folded envelope
in which he has caused to appear
her teeth and wedding ring.
His hand closes over mine.
His smile seems to require my approval
for his conjuring trick.

I feel inclined to applaud his skill
in so reducing flesh and bone
to this brief summary,
until I see his scuffed grey moccasins
and moth-eaten opera hat
with the folding mechanism showing through.

He takes me aside
and whispers that her ashes
will be waiting for me in Reception.
As we crunch back to the cars, we turn
and see smoke spiralling into the air,
while something difficult is imagined.

7 *i.m. M.V.*

You finally took the bait
You had cast some time before
You took the line in your mouth
You ran a mile or more

You hurled yourself in the air
You dived to the ocean floor
You came to the end of your breath
You wound yourself in to shore

Religion

If it were up to me
I would make use of sleep.
Going to church
would involve a flight of stairs
to a familiar bedroom,
where a broken alarm clock told the time.
The spreading of sheets,
the turning down of blankets,
would be followed by the drawing of curtains
in broad daylight,
the ritual of undressing.

Members of my religion
would be encouraged to sleep in
on Monday mornings
and any other morning they felt like it,
with no questions asked.
Sleep notes would be provided.
Couples would be authorised
to pull the covers over their heads
and spend their days tucked up
in cosy confessionals,
where all their sins would be forgiven.

Reckless Records

I wonder if this is my own copy
of *A Swingin' Affair!*
which I took to a party in 1961
and never saw again.
I was dancing with Belinda Davey,
the first one to speak to me
in that warm cheek language
of swaying on the spot
to 'I Won't Dance',
or 'Nice work if you can get it'.
I last saw the cover
of *A Swingin' Affair!*
lying on the carpet
of that Earls Court flat,
being trampled on
by twisting chukka boots.

I lost touch with Frank
for a few decades after that,
but *A Swingin' Affair!*
was always the best
of his Capitol albums
with the Nelson Riddle Orchestra –
better than the more famous
Songs for Swingin' Lovers!
which lost one of its best tunes
when it transferred to stereo.
Reckless Records are asking
about the same money I paid for it
the first time around –
scratched to ribbons of course,
but what do you expect?
I'll take it anyway.

Fur

I traced the makers
of his musquash-lined evening coat
from a label in the pocket
to a basement in Cork Street

and discussed repairing it with a man
who didn't remember my father
or the white waistcoats
they used to make for him before the war,

but smiled and shook his head
and suggested pulling out the fur
to sell separately
and offered me ten quid.

Embankment Gardens

I'm going out tonight in my black coat,
my front gleaming white.
I'm the last man in the world
to wear top hat and tails
to make his calls.
The ladies shout that I am hot.
I raise my hat to them.

What extraordinary beings
are let out after dark
to thrill and frighten us with their smiles.
I follow one to the kiosk where she works,
a hybrid creature
in gems and artificial fur,
who claws my face for me.

What was that snarl and fluster
up against a wall? What cried and shook
and tore itself apart?
I draw up the sides of my mouth
in the signal for pleasure.
My breath comes in plumes
along the Embankment Gardens.

Them

Just as you thought they had disappeared
forever out of your life, setting you free,
there they all were once more,
that just-fucked freshness clinging to their fur,
their tails curled into tight little knots
like dollops of whipped cream.

Notting Hill

Notting Hill Gate in the dead of winter.
A woman selling plantain bread.
A man who whispered,
'Sense, sense, sensomilia . . .
Don't you know what sensomilia is?'

He took our twenty quid
and disappeared down a side street,
leaving us with Geraldine,
his junkie teenage sidekick,
who said she hardly knew him.

Breakfast in Bed

How can she look at me this morning
after what I did to her last night?
I totally used her.
I made no attempt at foreplay.
I even forgot her name.
She was just a woman to me.

Now here she is this morning
looking at me with big eyes,
as if she expects breakfast in bed –
coffee, croissants and the Sunday papers –
and here I am putting on my coat
to fetch them for her.

A Pillow Book

to R.E.

I

I lie in bed, watching you
dress yourself in nudity
for your part in a story
you are about to tell me.

Once upon a time, you seem to say,
there was a woman who took off all her clothes
and stood for a moment
with one hand on her hip.

You have my full attention
as you pile your hair on top of your head
and let it fall down again.
Up to this point I am familiar with the story.

Your movements suggest a possible outline,
but nothing is certain yet.
You lift your arms above your head
in a gesture of boredom or surrender.

Your hands touch in mid-air
and you turn them palm-side-out
in a kind of question mark,
as you ask for help with the ending.

2

The story sets out along your limbs,
feeling its way forward
round the crook of a knee,
the angle of an elbow,

getting tangled in your hair.
It follows the line of your arms
as they cross one another
taking off your pullover,

or disappear behind your back.
It hovers round your shoulders,
touches on your breasts,
moves on to the whiteness

of your skin, the long flow
of your waist where it turns into
your hips. It has stripped you down
to the merest outline,

where everything makes sense.
I turn the pages more quickly now,
wanting and not wanting
the story's resolution.

3

This is the only kind of work
I'm any good at –
watching you take off your make-up
and put on moisturiser.

From toner to night cream
I check the progress
of these preparations
for shades of meaning and mood.

I can't be sure of anything
in our silent collaboration,
till you undress completely
and don't put on your nightdress.

I let the scene go on
for as long as it wants to,
knowing that soon you will be joining me
in the complications of the plot.

I open the book for you
and you slip between its pages –
the perfect illustration
to whatever happens next.

4

You can't find your hairbrush
or your hair band. It's too cold
to get undressed completely
tonight, do I mind?

You look at me suspiciously,
as if I might be
wearing pyjamas myself
under the covers.

I'm not saying anything
until I see everything
you are wearing
lying in a heap on the floor.

Oh dear, that was your last
pair of pants.
What are you going to do?
You might have to go home tomorrow.

I lie here as usual,
in thrall to the ritual,
knowing that all I have to do
is warm the bed for you.

5

Your top goes up,
your jeans come down,
your bra goes round to the side
while you undo the clasp.

What's left is a wisp
of something flowery,
slung between your hips
like a cocktail glass.

You tilt it this way and that,
till your movements displace
a ripple of soft porn
over the brim of the room.

I can't help noticing
the way you push your pants down
without bending your knees,
then kick them into a corner.

Of course, I could be wrong about this
and all that is really going on
is you undressing,
getting ready for bed.

6

You throw your things on a chair
and move about the room
with nothing on,
opening and closing drawers,

looking for something you've lost
among the bottles and jars
on your dressing table.
When you find it at last

you pour something in your hand
and rub it on your body,
as if you were
conjuring yourself from a lamp.

A blue flame springs up
where you were standing
and a chain reaction
sets out round the room.

I feel the heat of you on my face
as you pass in front of me.
Now your perfume takes over
the telling of our story.

7

I've heard it before, of course,
this bedtime story of ours
about two people in a room
and what happens next

in the pastoral scene
in the pattern of the wallpaper,
but every time it is new,
every time it is the same:

a woman undressing,
a man lying at her feet,
till there comes a point in the story
when you turn down the light.

I lie here watching you,
hoping you will go over the action
one more time,
to jog my memory.

How the plot twists and turns
on its toes, before revealing itself.
How the various storylines
come together finally.

8

And always the secret music
of your perfume
accompanying your entrance
on a stage at the foot of the bed.

Its sunflower colours
of pepper and honey
echo themes of resistance
and surrender

in a play you are putting on
for my improvement.
You stand on one leg,
tugging at one striped sock

that doesn't want to come off.
Opposing pieces of action
flow into one another,
then draw apart again.

I should understand by now
what you are saying or not saying,
but pepper and honey
have clouded my judgement.

9

One of our characters lacks
motivation tonight.
He's sulking slightly.
It's been a long day.

He gets into bed first
and pulls the covers up to his chin.
He might be asleep,
or he might only be pretending.

She might be undressing,
or she might be putting on her
nightdress, hoping for
a night's sleep herself.

The action slows
to a period of reflection,
sitting on the arm of a chair.
Her feet are killing her.

She can't make up her mind
what she feels about all this.
She glances round the room,
looking for a place to lie down.

Words reach out like hands
to hold you still,
as pictures of you undressing
fan out round the room.

You might be hanging up a shirt
behind the bedroom door,
treading your jeans underfoot
with a sulky look on your face,

or bending over
to put something away in a drawer.
You might be lifting up your arms
to put up your hair,

or looking in the bedside cupboard
for the moisturiser.
I should collect these images
to remember you by.

Each one pauses for a moment
to imprint itself on the air,
before slowly detaching itself
and disappearing forever.

All I have to do
is describe the scene to myself
and I am back there,
peering into the shadows.

It is a darkened room
where a sodium glow from the street
wanders under a blind
that won't pull all the way down.

You enter through a door on the right,
drying your hair,
laughing at one of your own jokes.
All I have to do

is watch while you explain
what is happening between us
in the language of undressing.
Are we naked tonight?

Or are we holding something back?
I don't mind, really I don't.
Nothing matters any more,
so long as we're together.

Is that you over there
in your nightdress,
standing on one leg,
looking at the sole of your foot?

It must be you
because all your things are still here –
face creams and cotton buds,
cleanser and eyeliner,

scattered across the table
where you put on make-up
and do your hair.
I know it is you

because you don't put the tops back
on the bottles. I do that.
I see you clearly now,
laughing at my fussiness,

or is that the ghost of you laughing?
You lean towards me,
holding your hands behind your back,
as if you are asking me to choose.

Depression Olympics

I was holding my head in my hand
like a shot-put or discus thrower.
I wasn't burying it in the sand,
I was holding my head in my hand.
I wondered where it would land
if I hurled it with all my power.
I was holding my head in my hand
like a shot-put or discus thrower.

In My Wildest Jeans

If these are the hollow eyes of 'mid maturity',
the map of veins beside the nose, the beard
showing up like iron filings underneath the skin,
then these must be the over-stuffed jeans
of material success, the ones with a zip
that shyly presents itself to the world,
a hint of underpants and vest
suggesting a breakthrough into seriousness.

Am I a better person now, with a fat arse,
flipflops and a back-support for the car?
In my wildest dreams I never looked like this.
I walked around like 'The Man from Laramie',
practising my cross-draw and return.
I leapt in the air and fell, clutching my stomach,
twitching occasionally. In my wildest dreams
I was only pretending to be dead.

King-Wilkinson

Tiny, old, completely bald,
yet strangely recognisable still
in his winter plumage – no,
not myself this time,
caught sight of in a mirror,
making me jump out of my skin,

but an old school friend
whose hand I used to hold,
advancing towards me across the room,
as across the years, saying:
'You remember me, don't you?
I used to be King-Wilkinson.'

You Have to Laugh

Well done for getting up!
Well done for getting dressed!
You can't work out what day of the week it is,
but the *Radio Times* will know. What's wrong
with buying two copies if you want to?
You strut up and down
with a disagreeable expression on your face.

You move forward in a series of little skids,
like hand-brake turns.
You have to laugh
when you see yourself clinging to banisters,
as if you were playing the harp.
You shuffle down the passage with a tray
and hit your head on something hard.

You come to a standstill in the hall.
Spots dance. Blood flows. A face
looks back at you which looks quite like
your own. You have to smile
when the mist clears
and you don't know where you are.
Perhaps a Lemsip would make you feel better?

You can't help using the word 'strange'
to describe your circumstances.
You glimpse little mad things everywhere,
for which only you can take credit.
You gesture at something you needed once,
over the back of something,
which can't be seen from here.

Marital Visit

The odd thing put away
in the wrong place – cups and plates
back in the cupboard
that I always leave out,
curtains open on the street
that I always keep drawn,
remind me of your recent brief
progress through here,
looking for something in the attic.

How could I forget:
butter in the fridge, but never eggs,
burnt matches everywhere,
in spite of the gas lighter,
jam jars soaking in water
to get the labels off.
How typical of you
to give the Chinese teapot a last chance
to prove itself in company.

And look at that tea towel
slung like your signature
over the back of a chair.
I could weep for the small spoons
lying down with the forks,
the corkscrew with the tea strainer.
Leave them where they are forever?
Or harden my heart
and put them back where they belong?

All the Cowboys' Horses

I lost hundreds of film stars, flowers,
the bird, not a magpie,
that steals brightly coloured things,
the cat-like animal
with a perfume sack on its neck.
I was trying to remember
who shouted out 'Wakey Wakey!'
Was it Arthur Askey?
The name of my favourite biscuit
melted on the tip of my tongue.

I forgot who it was
who took me up in a fighter plane
and gave me a medal for something.
I was best friends with one of his sons,
who had a racing bike
that wasn't a Raleigh.
We went to see *Shane* together,
starring someone like James Stewart.
We could reel off the names
of all the cowboys' horses.

Coup de Théâtre

The left-hand side of the stage
consists of a giant mousetrap
roughly disguised as a breakfast area.
A few pieces of furniture are scattered about
on the slightly raised trip-floor.
Instead of a piece of cheese on a spike
a table is laid for a meal.
A large spring is visible in the background.

Most of the action takes place
on the right-hand of the stage,
where people are sitting around talking.
Occasionally one of them will get up
and go over to the breakfast area,
but as soon as he sets foot on the trip-floor
an iron bar comes down out of the wings
and squashes him flat.

West End Final

He kept his make-up on all the time
towards the end, 'for the sake of economy',
Leichner 5 and 9 for indoor work,
red dots in the corners of his eyes.
'A word of praise for the Old Coachman,'
wrote *Plays and Players*.
'He only comes on in the last five minutes,
dripping wet, poor fellow,
but he makes the whole fantastic story
very real and pathetic . . .'
He would read that over to himself
to remind himself who he was.

His girlfriend, half his age,
thought he was the leading man.
He imagined her a virgin.
'I am like Kipling's trunkless elephant,'
he told me once, 'full of insatiable curiosity.'
Then he poured a bucket of water over himself
and went on stage crying out
that his mistress had been drowned.
I wish I knew where he'd gone
because he left his make-up tin behind
and a monogrammed coat-hanger
presented to him by the management.

Nothing in Particular

What do I miss?
I'll tell you what I miss –
the sun coming up,
colour starting,
a sort of yellow dust
or luminous moss
gathering round the edges
of table and chair,
everything soft as soft rain
some average morning
when an upstairs window
catches the sun
and a young woman
turns back into a room.
A telephone rings
and once again she clears her throat.
Nothing in particular,
words, desires,
the slightest intention
translated into action,
the chain of command
taking shape in the mind
according to logic and reason,
a tree coming into leaf,
our reward in heaven.

Washing My Hands

Muddy water comes clear
and I see my hands as they once were
with dirt under the fingernails.

I'm putting the finishing touches
to a tangle of branches and leaves
jammed between two rocks.

The dam seems to be holding,
the stream backing up, overflowing its banks.
I can take my hands away.